The new world of disruption, speed, and ongoing change is here. But you do not need to panic. Learning human superpowers will help you build the meta skills needed for individuals, teams, and organisations to thrive.

Get a free copy of a 30-minute course where you will learn more about the new world of work, how it affects organisations and individuals, and how to prepare yourself to thrive in it: http://aha.pub/NewWorldOfWork.

Knowing Your Superpowers Is the Key to Your Success in a Changing World

Building Personal Agility for More Success in Your Job and in Your Life

Marianne Roux

THiNKaha®

An Actionable Success Journal

E-mail: info@thinkaha.com
20660 Stevens Creek Blvd., Suite 210
Cupertino, CA 95014

Please go to
https://aha.pub/KnowingYourSuperpowers
to read this AHAbook and to share the
individual AHAmessages that resonate with you.

Published by THiNKaha®
20660 Stevens Creek Blvd., Suite 210,
Cupertino, CA 95014
https://thinkaha.com
E-mail: info@thinkaha.com

First Printing: May 2020
Hardcover ISBN: 978-1-61699-363-4   1-61699-363-4
Paperback ISBN: 978-1-61699-362-7   1-61699-362-6
eBook ISBN: 978-1-61699-361-0   1-61699-361-8
Place of Publication: Silicon Valley, California, USA
Paperback Library of Congress Number: 2020905752

Dedication

To my husband and daughter—you help me thrive every day.

How to Read a THiNKaha® Book

A Note from the Publisher

The AHAthat/THiNKaha series is the CliffsNotes of the 21st century. These books are contextual in nature. Although the actual words won't change, their meaning will every time you read one as your context will change. Be ready, you will experience your own AHA moments as you read the AHA messages™ in this book. They are designed to be stand-alone actionable messages that will help you think about a project you're working on, an event, a sales deal, a personal issue, etc., differently. As you read this book, please think about the following:

1. It should only take 15–20 minutes to read this book the first time out. When you're reading, write in the underlined area one to three action items that resonate with you.
2. Mark your calendar to re-read this book again in 30 days.
3. Repeat step #1 and mark one to three more AHA messages that resonate. They will most likely be different than the first time. BTW: this is also a great time to reflect on the AHA messages that resonated with you during your last reading.

After reading a THiNKaha book, marking your AHA messages, re-reading it, and marking more AHA messages, you'll begin to see how these books contextually apply to you. AHAthat/THiNKaha books advocate for continuous, lifelong learning. They will help you transform your AHAs into actionable items with tangible results until you no longer have to say AHA to these moments—they'll become part of your daily practice as you continue to grow and learn.

Mitchell Levy, Global Credibility Expert
publisher@thinkaha.com

THiNKaha®

Contents

Introduction

We are more distracted, rushed, and stressed than ever before. Disruptive times call for agile mindsets, behaviours, and tools that help us thrive rather than survive. To navigate this world effectively, we have to let go of the old and learn to become the best version of ourselves with skill and intention. There are evidence-based superpowers that we can all learn to become masters of our own journeys through complexity. We can leverage the mindsets, skills, and behaviours to do the work that robots cannot do.

This book is designed to help individuals, teams, and organisations develop the mindsets and skills to thrive in this world rather than feel overwhelmed and stressed by it.

Personal reinvention is the most important skill to build in the new world of work. You need to let go of who you are today and recreate yourself, as the world around you changes. #LifeIsChanging

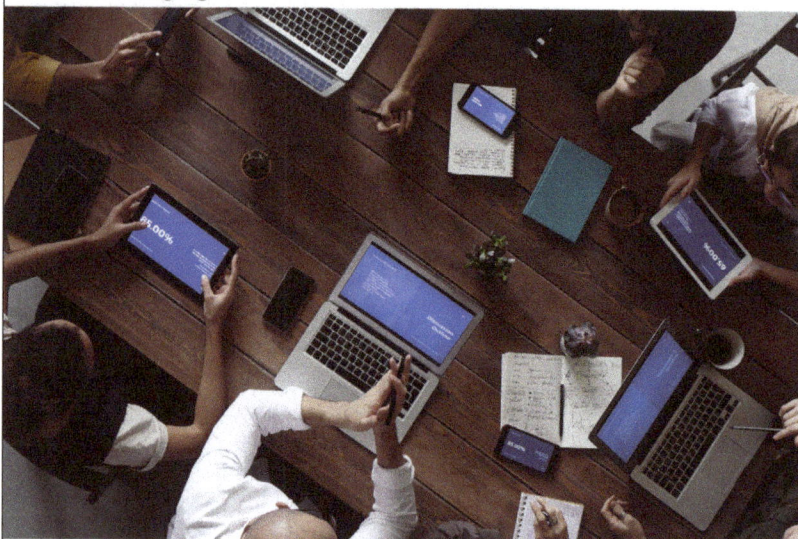

Marianne Roux
https://aha.pub/KnowingYourSuperpowers

Share the AHA messages from this book socially by going to
https://aha.pub/KnowingYourSuperpowers.

Section I

The World of Work Is Changing, and YOU Need to Change with It

In this world, where people are more distracted, rushed, and stressed than ever, you need to build mindsets, skills, and behaviours that help you and others thrive.

Luckily, there are evidence-based methods and tools which I call human superpowers that you can develop and use together to become the master of your own life and work journey.

Scan the QR code or use this link to watch the section videos:
https://aha.pub/KnowingYourSuperpowersSVs

1

The new world of work is technology-driven and complex. If you want to #Thrive, you need to step up and use your #Superpowers to become more complex yourself.

_____

_____

_____

2

Probably 40% of the world's leading companies will not exist in a meaningful way 10 years from now.
—John Chambers via https://aha.pub/MarianneRoux #LifeIsChanging

_____

_____

_____

3

Robots take jobs, not skills. New jobs will be created that need more human skills and new opportunities. #LifeIsChanging

_____

_____

_____

4

Personal reinvention is the most important skill to build in the new world of work. You need to let go of who you are today and recreate yourself, as the world around you changes. #LifeIsChanging

_____

_____

_____

5

To become the best version of yourself, you need to know your #Superpowers. These are your mindsets, skills, and behaviours that are the basis of all others and help you thrive in change and challenge.

_____

_____

_____

6

Sometimes, we fear our own greatness more than we fear our shortcomings. Don't let fear keep you from being the best version of yourself. #Superpowers

_____

_____

_____

7

People who are intentional and proactive are those who can survive and #Thrive in the new world of work. How aware are you of your mindsets and behaviours and how they affect your success?

_____

_____

_____

8

People have more access to information and learning now than ever. However, many of us don't spend the time to reflect and learn. You need to be a self-driven learner and reflect to #Thrive in the new world of work.

_____

_____

_____

9

Lifelong learning is the ongoing, voluntary, and self-motivated pursuit of knowledge. Are you a lifelong learner? You should be if you want to keep up in the changing world. #Thrive

_____

_____

_____

10

We are dependent learners. We often wait for others to provide us with learning opportunities and feed us with knowledge and opportunities. In this new world, you need to take charge of your learning and opportunities. #Thrive.

_____

_____

_____

11

If you want to help other people in today's world, you need to help yourself first. Using the plane analogy, put the oxygen mask on yourself first, then help others put theirs on. #Superpowers

_____

_____

_____

12

When you grow, you become more helpful to others by:
1) becoming a good role model for them and
2) sharing your learnings. #Superpowers

_____

_____

_____

13

Most of what you need to #Thrive in this new world
of work is already inside you. You need to
acknowledge your #Superpowers and work on it.

_____

_____

_____

You can shift from a fixed to a #GrowthMindset by changing your habits and language. Have a growth mindset in everything that you do.

Marianne Roux

https://aha.pub/KnowingYourSuperpowers

Share the AHA messages from this book socially by going to **https://aha.pub/KnowingYourSuperpowers**.

Section II

Superpower 01: Having a Growth Mindset

Do you believe that there are things you're not good at? That there are things you simply cannot learn because of your limitations? If your answer to both is yes, then you have what Carol Dweck calls a fixed mindset. This mindset will inhibit your ability to thrive in the new world of work.

Having the opposite, a growth mindset, will help you lean into the new challenges that await you. It will equip you to try new things and persevere. This is a core skill for a world where ongoing learning will be a game changer for individuals and organisations.

Scan the QR code or use this link to watch
the section videos:
https://aha.pub/KnowingYourSuperpowersSVs

14

The #GrowthMindset is the core mindset underpinning all others. It's a superpower of belief that you can learn anything if you put your mind to it. This mindset will help you thrive in the new world of work.

_____

_____

_____

15

With a #GrowthMindset, challenges are exciting rather than threatening. Instead of thinking, "Oh, I'm going to reveal my weakness!" say, "Wow! Here's a chance to grow."
—Carol Dweck via https://aha.pub/MarianneRoux

_____

_____

_____

16

Your mindset is a product of your language and habits. Develop habits and use language that give you a #GrowthMindset. Discover things you don't know yet. Always replace "no" with "not yet."

_____

_____

_____

17

Move from an "I can't" to an "I can" mindset. Believe that even if you don't know something—yet—you can always learn it. #GrowthMindset

_____

_____

_____

18

There can be times in your life when you start having fixed ideas about things, which can keep you from learning and growing. What are the things you have a fixed mindset on? #GrowthMindset

_____

_____

_____

19

A fixed mindset is the opposite of a #GrowthMindset. It is the belief that you can't do something and that you can never be good at it. Believe that you can be better.

_____

_____

_____

20

A fixed mindset is believing that 1) people can't learn, 2) people can't grow, and 3) people have to be told what to do. Do you have a fixed mindset? #GrowthMindset

_____

_____

_____

21

A fixed mindset is when you are arrogant about what you know. You think that what you know is the truth. This can hinder your growth and success. #GrowthMindset

_____

_____

_____

22

Love challenges, be intrigue by mistakes,
enjoy effort, and keep on learning.
—Carol Dweck via https://aha.pub/MarianneRoux

_____

_____

_____

23

Upbringing and schooling contribute to a fixed mindset.
There are parents and teachers who say, "You can never
be good at anything." But the truth is, you can be good at
anything if you put your mind to it. #GrowthMindset

_____

_____

_____

24

Be careful about toxic and narcissist people with no good intentions. Create a healthy distance and boundaries with that person. #GrowthMindset

_____

_____

_____

25

Having a fixed mindset can hold you back from developing yourself. Don't let it hold you back from becoming the best version of yourself. #GrowthMindset

_____

_____

_____

26

You can shift from a fixed to a #GrowthMindset by changing your habits and language. Have a growth mindset in everything that you do.

_____

_____

_____

27

Hear and interrupt your fixed mindset voice. —Carol Dweck via https://aha.pub/MarianneRoux #GrowthMindset

_____

_____

_____

28

If you are not open to learning and always give up when something is challenging, you can't grow. If you don't have a #GrowthMindset, you won't be able to keep up.

_____

_____

_____

29

To have a #GrowthMindset, you have to make it exciting for you to learn and grow. Every week, challenge yourself to do something new to keep those learning juices flowing.

_____

_____

_____

30

Having a #GrowthMindset culture can help your organisation deal with and thrive in the new technology-driven world of work.

_____

_____

_____

31

With a #GrowthMindset superpower, there's no limit to what you can learn and achieve. Not even the new world of work can stop you.

_____

_____

_____

#Grit is setting clear long-term goals and persevering in achieving those goals no matter what comes your way.

Marianne Roux
https://aha.pub/KnowingYourSuperpowers

Share the AHA messages from this book socially by going to
https://aha.pub/KnowingYourSuperpowers.

Section III

Superpower 02: Building Grit

Angela Duckworth's studies have helped us understand that there is more to success than IQ and physical strength. Grit—the right blend of passion and perseverance—has shown time and again to be the key differentiator of long-term success across several studies.

Grit means we are in it for the long haul. As Angela says: "Grit is living life like it's a marathon, not a sprint." Just like in a marathon, grit is the stamina that will keep you running towards your long-term goal despite difficulties and distractions. If you are gritty, nothing will stop you until you reach the finish line.

Scan the QR code or use this link to watch
the section videos:
https://aha.pub/KnowingYourSuperpowersSVs

32

#Grit is having the right blend of passion, perseverance, and resilience. It's a superpower that will help you achieve your long-term goals in the new world of work.

_____

_____

_____

33

Resilience is bouncing back after adversity and being adaptable. Perseverance is staying committed to learning or completing something. #Grit is sustaining interest and effort towards long-term goals using self-control.

_____

_____

_____

34

#Grit is living life like it's a marathon, not a sprint.
—Dr. Angela Lee Duckworth via
https://aha.pub/MarianneRoux

_____

_____

_____

35

#Grit is setting clear long-term goals and persevering in achieving those goals no matter what comes your way.

_____

_____

_____

36

#Grit is holding onto your long-term goals even when things come up and cause delays. Keep your goals in mind and keep moving forward, one step at a time.

_____

_____

_____

37

#Grit is about holding onto things that are really important to you, despite distractions and difficulties.

_____

_____

_____

38

#Grit is that ability to keep trying even when things don't go your way. The people who fail and keep trying are usually the grittiest.

_____

_____

_____

39

One of the things that take away #Grit is when you go after any shiny new thing and don't stay committed to your long-term goal.

_____

_____

_____

40

#Grit teaches you self-control and delayed gratification. This helps you have sustained interest and efforts towards your long-term goals.

_____

_____

_____

41

Having self-control means making the right choices on how you spend your time and whom you spend it with. They must all support your long-term goals. #Grit

_____

_____

_____

42

Having clear goals, passion, and perseverance is not enough to succeed if you don't have #Grit.

_____

_____

_____

43

Some people don't stick and persevere with one thing. They give up when it gets hard. This often stops people from being successful. #Grit

_____

_____

_____

44

People who have achieved great things in life definitely deferred short-term gratification and had self-control. #Grit

_____

_____

_____

45

To build #Grit, you've got to have real long-term goals that you keep working towards no matter what.

46

Sometimes, if things come too easy for you, you don't learn self-control and delayed gratification. Long-term and challenging goals can shape people to be grittier. #Grit

_____

_____

_____

47

It's not that I'm so smart.
It's just that I stay with problems longer.
—Albert Einstein
via https://aha.pub/MarianneRoux #Grit

_____

_____

_____

48

You can turn your interest into a purpose and a reality through discipline, self-control, and consistent practice. #Grit

_____

_____

_____

49

Angela Duckworth's work on building #Grit involves a 12-item questionnaire that reveals your grit score. This test can help you determine if you can make it or not.

_____

_____

_____

50

Excellence doesn't mean perfection; it means never giving in, never giving up, and ultimately, achieving the goal.
#Grit

_____

_____

_____

51

People with #Grit have a clear passion and the resiliency to get back up every time they get knocked down. This superpower can help you be headstrong as you face challenges in the new world of work.

_____

_____

_____

KNOW THYSELF

#SelfAwareness means having a grip on your thoughts and emotions. This superpower helps you translate thoughts and emotions into actions, which create your desired impact.

Marianne Roux

https://aha.pub/KnowingYourSuperpowers

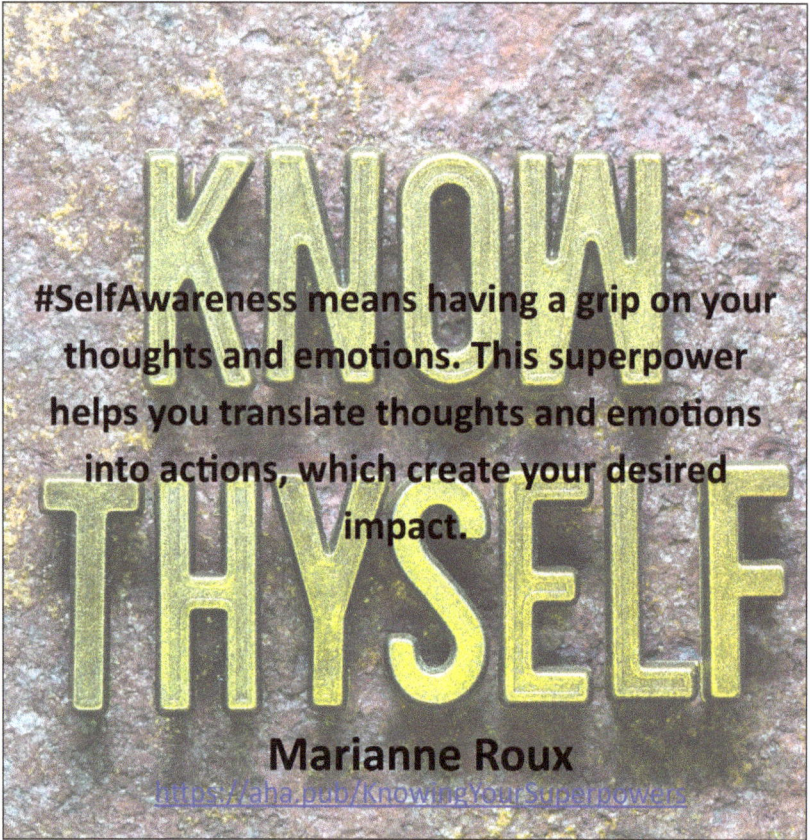

Share the AHA messages from this book socially by going to
https://aha.pub/KnowingYourSuperpowers.

Section IV

Superpower 03: Becoming More Self-Aware

We have known for a long time that self-awareness is a superpower that distinguishes individuals. When we know ourselves and how others see us, we can adjust our behaviour and emotions effectively and we are more approachable and confident. Most importantly, we can continually mature and grow.

Unlike grit and having a growth mindset, you will need feedback from those around you to develop this superpower. But once you attain self-awareness, you can identify your strengths and maximize them. Self-awareness can help you create the impact that you've always wanted to create.

Scan the QR code or use this link to watch
the section videos:
https://aha.pub/KnowingYourSuperpowersSVs

52

#SelfAwareness is a superpower in the new world of work. It's the ability to know yourself well and to keep learning.

_____

_____

_____

53

Half of the time we operate on autopilot or unconscious of what we are doing or how we feel, our mind wanders to somewhere else other than here and now. — Psychologists Matthew Killingsworth and Daniel T. Gilbert via https://aha.pub/MarianneRoux #SelfAwareness

_____

_____

54

#SelfAwareness means having a grip on your thoughts and emotions. This superpower helps you translate thoughts and emotions into actions, which create your desired impact.

_____

_____

_____

55

#SelfAwareness helps you align your intentions with your actions. When they are aligned, you can create your desired impact.

_____

_____

_____

56

A person who wants to be #SelfAware has to intentionally clean their inner life.

_____

_____

_____

57

#SelfAwareness helps you identify your strengths. When you know what you're good at, you can determine whether you are using your strengths well.

_____

_____

_____

58

Being #SelfAware includes understanding your strengths. You will feel much better about yourself if you work from your strengths.

_____

_____

_____

59

People with #SelfAwareness know which interactions work for them and which do not. They can decide which ones to retain and which ones to let go.

_____

_____

_____

60

#SelfAwareness requires cleaning your brain from the mental clutter. It involves casting out the negative self-talk from your system so you can judge yourself better.

_____

_____

_____

61

Being #SelfAware involves being open to information.
If you want to be #SelfAware, be flexible about the things
you need to make adjustments on.

_____

_____

_____

62

Part of #SelfAwareness is sitting down and analysing:
1) what worked for you, 2) what did not, and
3) what you don't like to take with you in the future.

_____

_____

_____

63

To achieve #SelfAwareness, ask your peers about:
1) what you did well, 2) what you didn't do well,
and 3) what you should have done differently.

_____

_____

_____

64

Getting feedback helps you become more #SelfAware.
It helps you see whether your actions generate
your desired impact.

_____

_____

_____

65

People judge themselves based on their intentions, while they judge others based on their actions. #SelfAwareness requires asking for feedback so you will know how others view your actions.

_____

_____

_____

66

Everyone in this world has blind spots. But a person with a low level of #SelfAwareness cannot see their own blind spots, while everyone around them can.

_____

_____

_____

67

Are you aware of your blind spots? Do you understand your thoughts and emotions well? Your answers to these questions will determine your level of #SelfAwareness.

_____

_____

_____

68

No person gets to the final point of #SelfAwareness. It's an ongoing process that you have to work on every single day.

_____

_____

_____

69

You have to keep working hard to achieve #SelfAwareness. It may not be easy, but you can make a choice to go for it every single day.

_____

_____

_____

70

#SelfAwareness will help you evolve continually into the best version of yourself. It's a behaviour that you need in the new world of work.

_____

_____

_____

71

When you are #SelfAware, you can say and do what is consistent with your values. You'll know yourself well. You can identify what's important for you in the new world of work.

_____

_____

_____

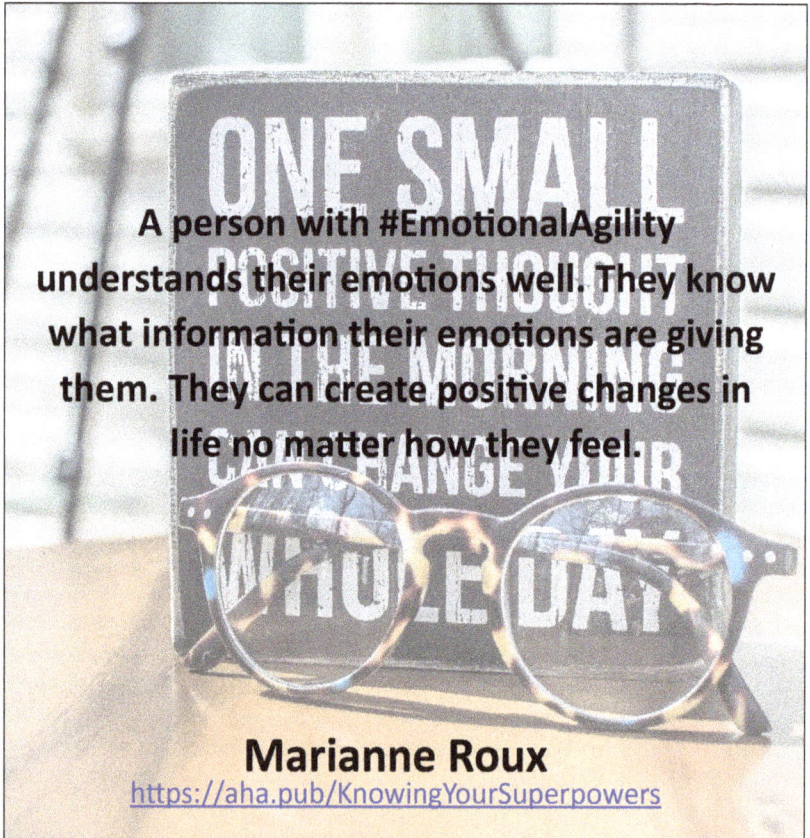

A person with #EmotionalAgility understands their emotions well. They know what information their emotions are giving them. They can create positive changes in life no matter how they feel.

Marianne Roux
https://aha.pub/KnowingYourSuperpowers

Share the AHA messages from this book socially by going to
https://aha.pub/KnowingYourSuperpowers.

Section V

Superpower 04: Leveraging Emotional Agility and Positivity

The bottom line of emotional agility is understanding all your emotions—negative and positive—and being able to align your decisions and actions intentionally. Emotional agility helps you see the possibilities despite your overwhelming emotions. It saves you from your brain's natural bias to negativity and helps you choose a more effective way forward. Together with emotional agility, emotional courage helps you lean into the emotions appropriately.

Positive psychologists also say that individuals are more empowered to make decisions and take actions when they have a more positive mindset. It is contagious, broadens what you see, and helps you have hope and perseverance in difficult situations.

Scan the QR code or use this link to watch
the section videos:
https://aha.pub/KnowingYourSuperpowersSVs

72

#EmotionalAgility is a superpower that will help you see things with the right perspective. It helps you think right, no matter how you feel, so you can properly respond to any situation in the new world of work.

_____

_____

_____

73

#EmotionalAgility is understanding your thoughts, emotions, and stories in ways that are compassionate, curious, and courageous.
—Susan David via https://aha.pub/MarianneRoux

_____

_____

_____

74

#EmotionalAgility is the ability to be with your thoughts and emotions without being blinded. It empowers you to see past your emotions and understand the information behind them.

_____

_____

_____

75

Part of #EmotionalAgility is emotional awareness. Emotional agility is being aware of your emotions, understanding them, and using them to be intentional about decisions and actions.

_____

_____

_____

76

#EmotionalAgility is not about converting a negative emotion into a positive one. It is understanding a negative feeling and being able to create an intentional and aligned outcome.

_____

_____

_____

77

Toxic positivity tells you to be happy all the time even when things are not fine. It invalidates an authentic human experience. This is not #EmotionalAgility.

_____

_____

_____

78

Each day, our brains keep track of our positive and negative moments. The resulting score contributes to our overall mood. Endeavour to move the proportion closer to the ideal of 5.6 positive to 1 negative.
—Barbara Fredrickson https://aha.pub/MarianneRoux

_____

_____

_____

79

A person with #EmotionalAgility understands their emotions well. They know what information their emotions are giving them. They can create positive changes in life no matter how they feel.

_____

_____

_____

80

People who are #EmotionallyAgile are hopeful realists. They face the facts, good and bad, but they are hopeful that they can sort it out.

_____

_____

_____

81

You have to be #EmotionallyAgile because only 7 of the top 22 emotions are positive. Doubt, worry, anger, fear, and other insecurities overwhelm passion, optimism, and other positive emotions.

_____

_____

_____

82

The human brain is set up to have a natural negativity bias. A person is inclined to think more about what can go wrong. #EmotionalAgility helps you adjust.

_____

_____

_____

83

A negative emotion can give you good information about your values. But you have to counter your brain's natural bias to negativity. Harness #EmotionalAgility so you can balance your experience.

_____

_____

_____

84

Human beings usually remember the negative things much more than the positive. A person with #EmotionalAgility understands their emotions better. They can direct their minds towards the positive.

_____

_____

_____

85

People are more affected emotionally and do more mental work from a single negative piece of feedback than from a single positive piece of feedback. It takes conscious effort to focus on the possible. #EmotionalAgility

_____

_____

_____

86

Being aware of your biases and cues will help you develop #EmotionalAgility. When you know your biases and cues, you can understand your emotions better. You will know how they affect you.

_____

_____

_____

87

Develop #EmotionalAgility by being conscious of situations when you are more biased on the negative. When you are conscious, you can guide your emotions better.

_____

_____

_____

88

Don't be scared of your emotions. Look at them with courage and curiosity. They can give you info that will turn you into the best version of yourself. #EmotionalAgility

_____

_____

_____

89

You have to 1) accept, 2) deal with, and 3) understand all your emotions, negative or positive. If you do, you can create an intentional result out of them. #EmotionalAgility

_____

_____

_____

90

#EmotionalAgility is a superpower that machines will find the hardest to imitate. In the new world of work, you need to develop this superpower. Understand the information your emotions are giving you, and use it to be more intentional in your responses.

_____

_____

_____

91

When you have the superpower of #EmotionalAgility, you can be more positive and hopeful. You can be more gritty and more self-aware and have a higher growth mindset in the new world of work.

_____

_____

_____

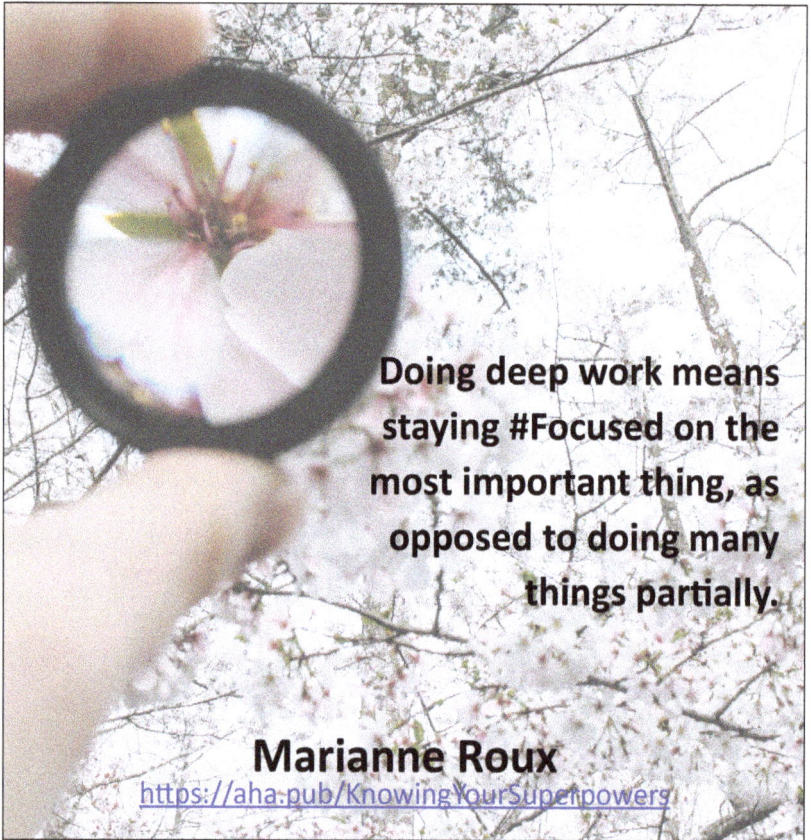

Doing deep work means staying #Focused on the most important thing, as opposed to doing many things partially.

Marianne Roux
https://aha.pub/KnowingYourSuperpowers

Share the AHA messages from this book socially by going to
https://aha.pub/KnowingYourSuperpowers.

Section VI

Superpower 05: Becoming More Focused

We all behave as if we have attention deficit disorder, tensely distracted by emails, text messages, and co-workers and unable to get out of constant non-value-adding meetings and tasks. In this section, you will learn about the brain-damaging effects of distraction and the attention residue that is created every time you move between tasks. Cal Newport and Nir Eyal in their books, *Deep Work* and *Indistractable* help us redefine our focus and attention to ensure that we spend more time on value-adding activities and less in shallow, distracted mode.

This skill will help you cope with increasingly complex problems and situations and help you learn new things faster. Being focused is a superpower that will make you more productive and thus deliver high-quality work faster. It will also increase the quality of your interactions with others through increased presence.

Scan the QR code or use this link to watch
the section videos:
https://aha.pub/KnowingYourSuperpowersSVs

92

We have created a society where people are more distracted than ever. Being #Focused is a superpower that will help you become productive in the very distracting new world of work.

93

When you are #Focused, you are more productive because you can do deep work.

94

Doing deep work means staying #Focused on the most important thing, as opposed to doing many things partially.

_____

_____

_____

95

Most people can do two 90-minute bursts of deep work a day. Taking a 15-minute break in between greatly improves #Focus.

_____

_____

_____

96

When you are #Focused on deep work,
you 1) perform better, 2) learn more easily,
and 3) produce better outcomes.

_____

_____

_____

97

There is an #AttentionResidue when you move between
tasks. When you check your phone or email while
working, it will take a couple more minutes to return
your #Focus to work.

_____

_____

_____

98

Moving between tasks leads to #AttentionResidue, which results in: 1) longer time at work, 2) worse outcomes, and 3) slower learning.

_____

_____

_____

99

Multitasking, by itself, is bad for your brain. When you multitask, your brain gets addicted to shallow work, and you lose the ability to stay #Focused.

_____

_____

_____

100

Multitasking is a result of giving in to distractions.
A person's dependence on distractions can be eliminated
if they are intentional on where they put their #Focus.

_____

_____

_____

101

Psychological research shows that a person who
multitasks makes more mistakes compared
to someone who is #Focused on one task.

_____

_____

_____

102

Most people in the new world of work feel frazzled.
They jump between tasks and interactions and feel they
are not getting real work done. This habit of not being
#Focused does not lead to a good outcome.

_____

_____

_____

103

It's hard to stay #Focused because we live in a society
where people are 1) impatient, 2) constantly feeling
rushed, and 3) unable to sustain attention.

_____

_____

_____

104

Most executives have symptoms of ADHD, which makes it hard for them to #Focus. One symptom of learnt ADHD is the persistent feeling of urgency. They can't identify what's urgent and what's a mere distraction.

_____

_____

_____

105

Distraction starts from within. Cultivate the ability to #Focus intensely on what you are doing.
—Nir Eyal via https://aha.pub/MarianneRoux

_____

_____

_____

106

Identify your distractions and decide to reduce and minimise them. Identify the most important thing that you need to #Focus on and decide to do deep work on it.

_____

_____

_____

107

Become aware of what makes you feel strong, energised, and engaged and what makes you feel weak, drained, and bored. Do more of the first and less of the second. #Focus

_____

_____

_____

108

It will be easier to #Focus if you manage your energy wisely. Know what part of the day you have the highest energy, and do deep work at that time.

_____

_____

_____

109

What you choose to #Focus on and what you
choose to ignore plays a big role in defining the
quality of your own life and that of others.
—Cal Newport via https://aha.pub/MarianneRoux

_____

_____

_____

110

#Focus is an essential superpower to becoming
productive in the new world of work. Shift from
multitasking to doing deep work. Focused deep work
leads to a productive you.

_____

_____

_____

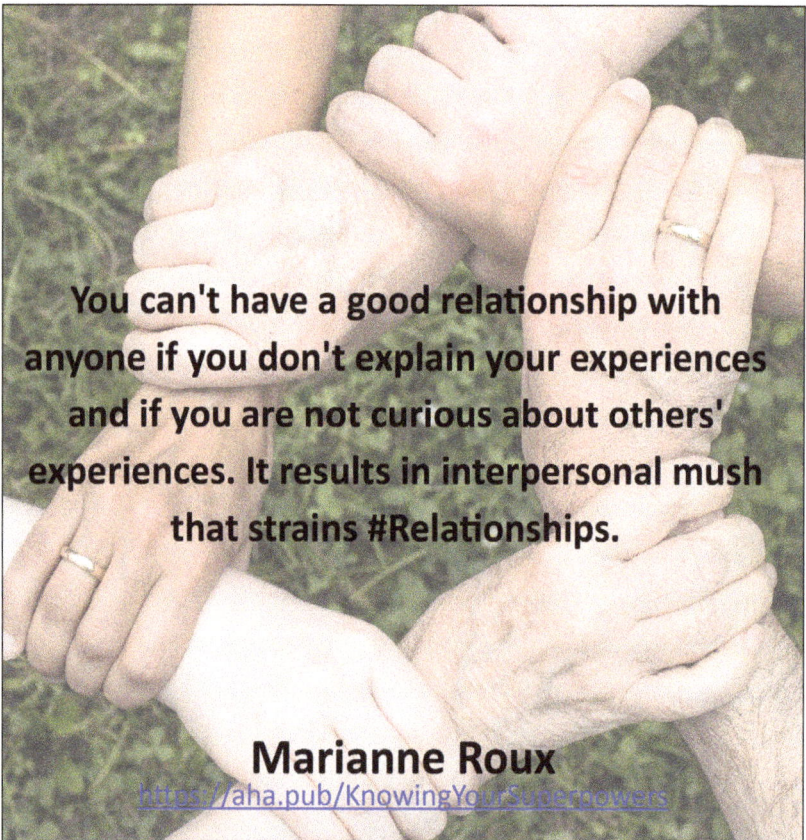

You can't have a good relationship with anyone if you don't explain your experiences and if you are not curious about others' experiences. It results in interpersonal mush that strains #Relationships.

Marianne Roux

https://aha.pub/KnowingYourSuperpowers

Share the AHA messages from this book socially by going to
https://aha.pub/KnowingYourSuperpowers.

Section VII

Superpower 06: Having Clear Relationships and Communication

Our relationships are, in the words of Professor Gervase Bushe, characterised by interpersonal mush as we try and make sense of events and others, but we never check out our own and others' stories. This lack of clear communication leads to conflict and misunderstanding.

To have clear communications and therefore, more positive relationships, you need to discover and validate what other people around you observe, feel, think, and want.

In this section, you will learn how to have interpersonal clarity with others through empathy, so you can respond in more constructive ways. You will also learn how to avoid the power triangle and work from an empowerment stance. Learn and apply the superpower of clear and positive relationships, and see how it will take your impact to the next level.

Scan the QR code or use this link to watch the section videos:
https://aha.pub/KnowingYourSuperpowersSVs

111

Having clear #Relationships and #ClearCommunication is a superpower that can help you navigate and thrive in the new world of work.

_____

_____

_____

112

Lack of #ClearCommunication leads to what Prof. Gervase Bushe calls an "interpersonal mush." It happens when you don't explain your experience to others, yet you assume that they understand it.

_____

_____

_____

113

We think that other people create our experiences. We assume that they are responsible for our happiness or sadness. Yet we are responsible for our own experiences. #Relationships

_____

_____

_____

114

You can't have a good relationship with anyone if you don't explain your experiences and if you are not curious about others' experiences. It results in interpersonal mush that strains #Relationships.

_____

_____

_____

115

Proper #Communication of experiences clears interpersonal mush. Explaining your experiences to others and listening to their stories leads to better #Relationships.

_____

_____

_____

116

Constant interpersonal mush harms relationships and wellbeing. Have clear #Communication and go for deeper #Relationships. They can improve your well-being and immune system.

_____

_____

_____

117

Our brain depends on mutual stimulation and beneficial interactions with others for its survival. Without it, neurons die! #ClearCommunications

_____

_____

_____

118

A person's own stories about themselves are always more positive, while their stories about others are more negative. #ClearCommunication is important to correct these stories in our heads.

_____

_____

_____

119

We achieve #ClearCommunications when we share our obserations, thoughts, emotions, and wants with each other regularly.

_____

_____

_____

120

David Rock's research shows that all of us have one of the five types of brain responses to #Communication: 1) status, 2) certainty, 3) autonomy, 4) relatedness, and 5) fairness. Know the brain response of the person you're talking to.

_____

_____

121

When you understand people's brain responses, you can #Communicate with them in such a way that increases rewards and reduces threats.

_____

_____

_____

122

A human brain is designed to be ready for #Relationships. It is evolutionarily designed to adjust to another person's perspectives and emotions. #Empathy

_____

_____

_____

123

Avoid the drama triangle of victim, rescuer, and persecutor behaviours. Work in the empowerment triangle of creator, challenger, and coach to create and maintain healthy #Relationships.
—Dr. Stephen Karpman
via https://aha.pub/MarianneRoux

124

Empathy is critical. Learning how to validate versus invalidate people is an important skill in the new world of work. Give others a chance to #Communicate their thoughts and emotions. Truly listen to them when they do.

125

Enjoy clearer #Communications and #Relationships through empathy. When you take time to listen and understand people, you can have interpersonal clarity with them.

_____

_____

_____

126

Clear #Communications and deep #Relationships lead to healthier and better outcomes for yourself and others. It's a superpower that will help you achieve interpersonal clarity with others in the new world of work.

_____

_____

_____

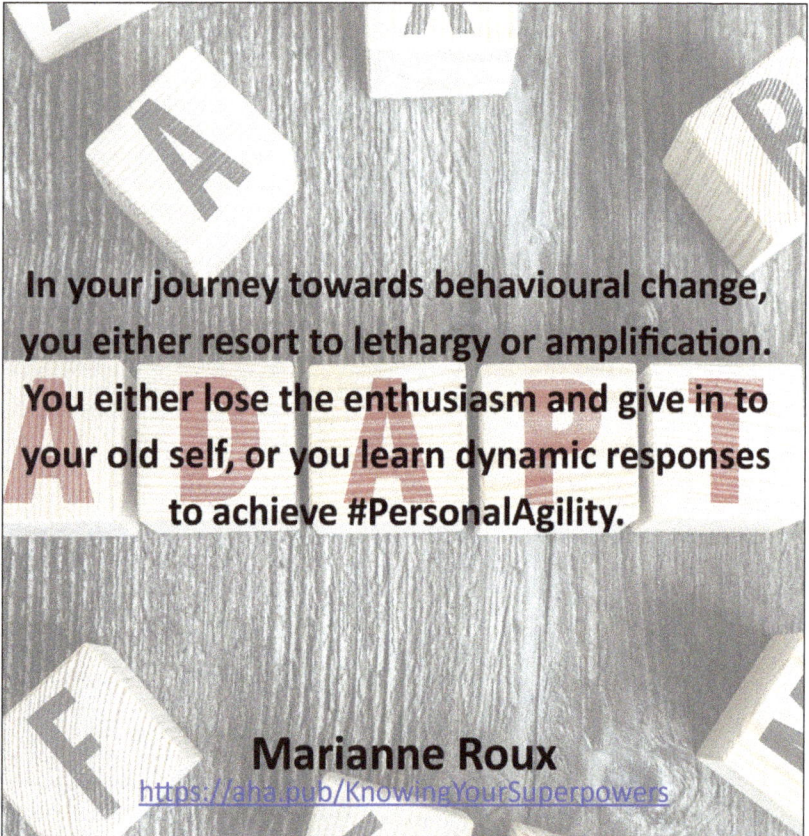

In your journey towards behavioural change, you either resort to lethargy or amplification. You either lose the enthusiasm and give in to your old self, or you learn dynamic responses to achieve #PersonalAgility.

Marianne Roux

https://aha.pub/KnowingYourSuperpowers

Share the AHA messages from this book socially by going to
https://aha.pub/KnowingYourSuperpowers.

Section VIII

Maintaining Personal Agility

You now understand the six human superpowers that you need in order to learn and thrive in the new world of work. But you should be warned: Behaviour and mindset change is not easy. It takes time. Expect your old habits and new obstacles to come up as you try to develop the superpowers that you've just learned. Also, don't expect everyone around you to like the change they'll see.

That makes this section the most important of all. It covers how you can embed these six mindsets, skills, and behaviours. Most importantly, this last section will teach you how to maintain personal agility throughout your life.

Scan the QR code or use this link to watch
the section videos:
https://aha.pub/KnowingYourSuperpowersSVs

127

Change is not going to happen overnight.
Maintain #PersonalAgility by developing these
superpowers: 1) growth mindset, 2) grit,
3) self-awareness, 4) emotional agility, 5) focus,
and 6) clear relationships and communication.

128

When faced with continual complexity at unprecedented
pace, your survival instincts kick in. You may act before
thinking. #PersonalAgility is needed in order to respond
smarter. https://aha.pub/McKinseyAndCompany

129

In your journey towards behavioural change, you either resort to lethargy or amplification. You either lose the enthusiasm and give in to your old self, or you learn dynamic responses to achieve #PersonalAgility.

_____

_____

_____

130

Behavioural change has five stages: 1) No, that's not me; 2) Maybe that's me; 3) Okay, what do I do now?; 4) Let's do it; and 5) I can see that it's possible. Maintaining #PersonalAgility involves going through them over and over.

_____

_____

_____

131

As you try to maintain #PersonalAgility, Kegan and Lahey urge us to look at your current habits and commitments. They may be stopping you from developing the behaviour that you're trying to achieve.

_____

_____

_____

132

If you want to maintain #PersonalAgility, figure out the hidden competing commitments in your life. They can hinder you in achieving behavioural change.

_____

_____

_____

133

You will be immune to change if you don't to let go of hidden competing commitments. Open yourself up to change so you can maintain #PersonalAgility.

_____

_____

_____

134

Establish your intention to achieve #PersonalAgility.
Check your calendar. Look at your actions. Revisit your
interactions. Are they aligned with your intention?
If not, change them. #PersonalAgility.

_____

_____

_____

135

Your habits will resist change as you try to maintain
#PersonalAgility. Fight this resistance and keep
moving forward.

_____

_____

_____

136

Walk towards the discomfort as you learn and maintain #PersonalAgility. It's okay if it's not comfortable. Discomfort is a sign that you are growing.

_____

_____

_____

137

When you are tempted to go back to your old habits, remind yourself to have a growth mindset. Amplify your desire to learn. Keep moving forward. #PersonalAgility

_____

_____

_____

138

The number of repetitions of the new behaviour before it becomes a habit is enormous. You don't do it one, two, or three times. You have to keep repeating it until it becomes a habit.
—James Clear via https://aha.pub/MarianneRoux
#PersonalAgility

139

You are allowed to be a masterpiece and a work in progress, simultaneously.
—Sophia Bush via https://aha.pub/MarianneRoux
#PersonalAgility

140

The new world of work calls for agile mindsets, behaviours, and tools that help you thrive rather than survive. Become a master of your journey by maintaining your superpowers. #PersonalAgility

_____

_____

_____

Appendix

Tools, Techniques, and YouTube Clips

TOOLS & TECHNIQUES

- VIA strengths finder — https://www.viacharacter.org
- Self awareness test — Tasha Eurich
- Interrupting the fixed mindset voice
- 4 step emotional agility exercise — Susan David
- Self differentiation — Gervase Bushe
- The Experience Cube — Gervase Bushe
- SCARF — David Rock
- Immunity to change map — Kegan and Lahey
  — https://www.youtube.com/watch?v=FFYnVmGu9Zl (15 min)
- The 12 item grit questionnaire — Angela Duckworth
- Positive to negative ratio
  — https://www.youtube.com/watch?v=_hFzxfQpLjM (8:45)
- Perspective taking — CCL
- Drama vs empowerment triangle — Karpman
  — https://www.youtube.com/watch?v=E_XSeUYa0-8 (6 min)
- Deep work — Cal Newport
- Timeboxing — https://www.youtube.com/watch?v=mtmXwuZ2ED8 (8:33)
- Gratitude journal
- Best possible self writing exercise

YOUTUBE CLIPS

- https://www.youtube.com/watch?v=pN34FNbOKXc The Power of belief — mindset and success | Eduardo Briceno |
- https://www.youtube.com/watch?v=_Ky-mKuhKgU Simon Sinek: 1:20 Reflect to grow
- Susan David on Emotional Agility
  — https://www.youtube.com/watch?v=0_6hu6JLH98 (6:55)
- https://www.youtube.com/watch?time_continue=1&v=1Evwgu369Jw Brene Brown — The power of empathy

- Angela Duckworth TED talk on Grit — https://www.ted.com/talks/angela_lee_duckworth_grit_the_power_of_passion_and_perseverance/transcript?language=en
- https://www.youtube.com/watch?v=Z7dFDHzV36g Barbara Fredrickson: Positive Emotions Open Our Mind (8:37)
- Cal Newport youtube clip on Deep Work — 6 min https://www.youtube.com/watch?v=zfoCyFvADtU
- Daniel Goleman youtube clip on Focus vs Frazzle — 7 min https://www.youtube.com/watch?v=Nexy76Jtu24
- Gervase Bushe — how to practice clear leadership — (10:29) https://www.youtube.com/watch?v=OBzttEvFUmE

Phrases and Words in Lexicon

- New world of work
- Reskilling, upskilling, and meta skilling
- Lifelong learning
- Personal agility
- Inside-out
- Habit change
- Beliefs
- Perspective
- Behaviour automaticity
- Brain plasticity
- Fixed mindset
- Growth mindset
- Grit
- Resilience
- Perseverance
- Passion
- Practice
- Purpose
- Hope
- Focus
- Deep work
- Time boxing
- Self awareness
- Self differentiation
- Choice
- Personal mastery
- Emotional agility
- Negativity bias
- Positivity
- Toxic positivity
- Contagious feelings
- Gratitude
- Clear relationships
- Interpersonal mush
- Drama triangle
- Empowerment triangle
- SCARF
- Triangulation
- Empathy
- Immunity to change

Bibliography

Chambers, J. (2016, March) Personal Interview with Rik Kirkland of McKinsey Publishing.

Carol Dweck, *Mindset: The New Psychology of Success* (Ballantine Books, December 26, 2007)

Dr. Angela Duckworth, *Grit: The Power of Passion and Perseverance* (Scribner, May 3, 2016)

Matthew A. Killingsworth and Daniel T. Gilbert, *A Wandering Mind Is an Unhappy Mind* (Science 330, 932 (2010), 12 November 2010)

Susan David, *Emotional Agility: Get Unstuck, Embrace Change, and Thrive in Work and Life* (Penguin Audio, September 06, 2016)

Barbara L. Fredrickson, *The Role of Positive Emotions in Positive Psychology*

The Broaden-and-Build Theory of Positive Emotions (American Psychologist, 56(3), 218–226, 2001)

Cal Newport *Deep Work: Rules for Focused Success in a Distracted World Hardcover* (Grand Central Publishing, January 5, 2016)

Nir Eyal, *Indistractable: How to Control Your Attention and Choose Your Life* (Bloomburry, 2019)

Prof. Gervase R. Bushe, *Clear Leadership: Sustaining Real Collaboration and Partnership at Work* (Nicholas Brealey; Revised Edition, May 13, 2010)

Karpman, Stephen B. M.D. *The New Drama Triangles.* USATAA/ITAA Conference Lecture, August 11, 2007

Robert Kegan and Lisa Laskow Lahey, *Immunity to Change: How to Overcome It and Unlock the Potential in Yourself and Your Organization (Leadership for the Common Good)* (Harvard Business Review Press, January 13, 2009)

Charles Duhigg, *The Power of Habit: Why We Do What We Do in Life and Business* (Duhigg, Charles; Reprint edition, 7 January 2014)

Kevin Cashman, *Leadership from the Inside Out: Becoming a Leader for Life* (ReadHowYouWant; 16th ed. Edition, December 28, 2012)

Daniel Goleman, *Focus: The Hidden Driver of Excellence* (Harper Paperbacks; Reprint edition, May 5, 2015)

About the Author

Marianne Roux is the founder and director of Roux Consulting (https://www.marianneroux.com/) and an associate at several business schools around the world. She has over 25 years of experience as a New World of Work strategist, leadership educator, transformation consulting director, and HR executive.

Marianne is a regular keynote speaker and author. She was chosen as one of 52 Inspirational Women at Work in South Africa in 2004 and one of 20 Female Entrepreneurs by Management Today in 2011 in Australia.

AHAthat®

THiNKaha has created AHAthat for you to share content from this book.

- ➲ Share each AHA message socially:
  https://aha.pub/KnowingYourSuperpowers
- ➲ Share additional content: **https://AHAthat.com**
- ➲ Info on authoring: **https://AHAthat.com/Author**

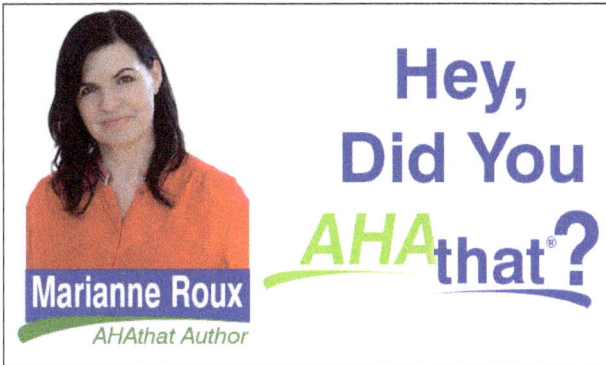

Marianne Roux
AHAthat Author

Hey, Did You AHAthat®?